RACHAEL NARINS

CAST-IRON
COOKING

RECIPES & TIPS
for Getting the Most out of Your
Cast-Iron Cookware

Storey Publishing

In memory of my brother, Joshua Narins

The mission of Storey Publishing is to serve our customers by
publishing practical information that encourages
personal independence in harmony with the environment.

Edited by Margaret Sutherland and Sarah Guare
Art direction and book design by Jeff Stiefel
Indexed by Christine R. Lindemer, Boston Road Communications

Cover photography by Mars Vilaubi (front) and © Keller + Keller Photography
(back); Rachael Narins photo courtesy of the author

Interior photography by © Keller + Keller Photography except: © Afripics/Alamy
Stock Photo, 9 bottom left; © Ari Nouslainen/123RF, 8 bottom; Mars Vilaubi, 7, 9
top left & right and bottom right; © Martin Darley/agefotostock.com, 8 top right

Endpapers created by Jeff Stiefel

Storey Publishing
210 MASS MoCA Way
North Adams, MA 01247
www.storey.com

Printed in China by Toppan Leefung Printing Ltd.
10 9 8 7 6 5 4 3 2 1

LIBRARY OF CONGRESS CATALOGING-IN-PUBLICATION DATA ON FILE

CONTENTS

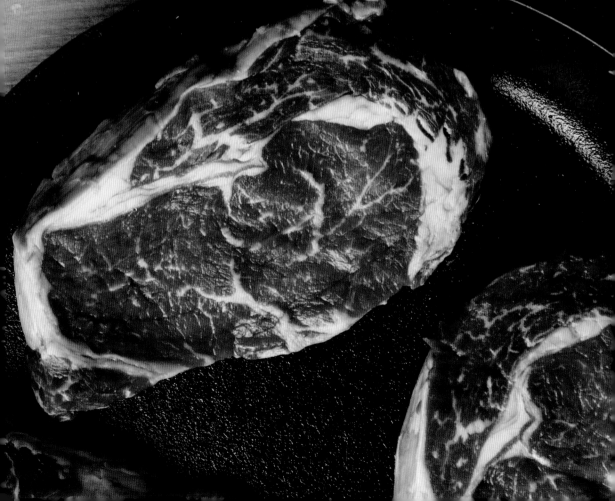

INTRODUCTION

All across America, there are cast-iron pans displayed proudly on pot racks in kitchens, decoratively hung from nails in barns, nestled in cupboards, and tucked away in attics and basements.

There are pans that are used daily and with love and pans that are waiting to be taken home from the shop or simply reclaimed. They are for sale everywhere, from the finest cookware shops to the funkiest flea markets. With price tags that range from under $20 to well over $200, there's a pan out there for every wallet.

Cast-iron pans hold memories of meals cooked and of families gathered. They can last for generations, so even the most neglected just need some attention and they're ready to get back to work.

A cast-iron pan is easy to use, easy to care for, and easy to love.

WHY AND HOW TO BUY CAST IRON

You may already have a set of cast-iron cookware, or you may be asking yourself, why should I invest in a cast-iron pan? For that matter, why invest in a cast-iron pan cookbook?

The unique properties of cast iron make it ideal for baking, sautéing, frying, slow cooking, and more. A well-made pan is virtually indestructible and when properly seasoned is nonstick. Iron is almost endlessly recyclable, so not only will it last you a lifetime, but you can feel good knowing it never has to end up in a landfill. A good pan will also add trace amounts of iron — a necessary nutrient — to your diet.

Cast iron heats slowly and holds that heat. It's a bit of a myth that it holds heat evenly, though. The pan will always be hotter directly over the burner. (You can sprinkle some flour in your pan and place it on a burner to see. The flour will darken first where the pan gets hottest.) To remedy this, consider purchasing a heat diffuser.

Recipes that are designed for cast iron take into account slower heating times and longer heat retention. Where glass will keep your baked goods light, cast iron is the choice for when you want a screaming hot pan for searing or a terrific golden crust.

The pans work on gas and electric stoves. They can go in the oven and can be used on induction burners and direct heat; outdoors, too, on a grill, hearth, or open fire. Many recipes in this book include directions for outdoor cooking.

At the most basic level, a cast-iron pan is just that: a pan made of iron that was cast in sand-blast molds, then polished. The tools have been slightly upgraded, but the manufacturing technique is the same as it has been for hundreds of years.

When buying cast iron, you will notice that there's only one major manufacturer left in America: Lodge. However, there are several very popular vintage brands you can buy online or find at garage sales or thrift shops. Happily, there are also at least two small — very small; they have waiting lists for their pans — craftsmen making pans to order: Finex in Portland, Oregon, and Borough Furnace in Syracuse, New York. They are worth seeking out.

Whether you decide to buy a brand-new pan or go with something vintage, think about what shapes and sizes you need. For the purposes of this book, you should have a 10- and a 12-inch skillet and 5- and 8-quart Dutch ovens (if you can only buy one size of each, go with the larger choices). Always consider the weight of a pan when purchasing. If it's too heavy to pick up, you aren't going to use it.

Collectors of vintage pots and pans look for certain manufacturers, such as Griswold. The beauty of collecting cast iron is that your investment isn't just for show; it can be used and treated like any other cast-iron pan in your kitchen.

SHASES & SIZES

Cast iron comes in a variety of shapes and sizes. Here are some of the most common, and a few uncommon options.

Skillet. Also known as a frying pan, a skillet has a handle, a wide cooking surface, and low sides. It's ideal for sautéing, searing, pan frying, broiling, and some baking.

Grill pan. This is a skillet with raised ridges inside the pan that add the look of grill marks to cooked food. The benefit to a grill pan is that whatever you put in it isn't going to cook in its own fat or moisture. The drawback is that this pan will need to be reseasoned more often than a flat-bottom pan, since sauces and fats pool in the grooves, requiring additional cleaning that often takes off the seasoning.

Dutch oven. A large, deep pot with a tight-fitting lid, a Dutch oven is sometimes called a cocotte or casserole dish. It can be round, oval, or heart-shaped, and some are made with legs for outdoor use. Dutch oven sizes are typically measured in quarts. The recipes in this book that serve four to six people work best in a 5-quart pot; use an 8-quart pot for larger recipes. The recipes in this book were written for seasoned, raw iron pans, but for the most part they can be made in enameled cast iron as well. You can cook acidic foods and boil water in enameled cast iron, which are not recommended in seasoned cast iron.

Stovetop accessories. Many stoves offer the option of a cast-iron grill or griddle, custom built to fit over an oval-shaped burner in the center of the stove top. These, too, need to be seasoned and treated the same as any other piece of cast-iron cookware.

Griddle. This is a rectangular flat surface, with grilling ridges on one side. It is designed to rest over two or more burners and is perfect for making multiple pancakes or fried eggs. The grill side is ideal for steaks, burgers, and whole vegetables.

Outdoor pots. All well-seasoned cast iron can be used outdoors, but some pots are designed specifically for grills, hearths, and campfires. They can come in sizes up to 40 gallons and typically have legs or a handle for hanging. These pots can be found online and at agricultural and farming supply stores. Enameled cast iron should be avoided.

Specialty pans. There are a few novelty cast-iron pans on the market. The classics are the æbleskiver pan (for creating the round, Danish popover-style doughnut) and the corn stick mold, but you can also find pans divided into wedges for corn bread, or in the shape of a cactus, and there's one midwestern artist making pans in the shape of all 50 states.

HOW TO SEASON CAST IRON

When you first acquire a new, unseasoned pan, wash it with warm soapy water, then dry it completely. Water will cause it to rust.

You then need to season your pan to create the nonstick surface. While the surface will resist sticking, it will never be as slick as Teflon, so you may want to use a touch of oil when cooking some foods, such as eggs, until the pan has had time to build a tough coating.

To season your pan:

1. Lightly oil the pan with organic vegetable oil. Wipe out any excess oil.

2. Place a foil-lined baking sheet on the lower rack of your oven (to catch any drips) and place the pan on the higher rack. Heat to 350°F/175°C and let the pan "bake" for 1 hour. Then turn off the heat and let the pan cool in the oven completely. That's it.

3. Repeat this process whenever food residue is not releasing easily or there are noticeable gray areas on the surface of the pan.

SEASONED VS. ENAMELED CAST IRON

The materials that cookware is made from have an effect on the resulting dish. For instance, if you bake a pie in glass, it will not brown the same way as it would if you bake it in a dark metal tin. The recipes in this book were written to be made in seasoned cast iron, which is dark, porous, and able to withstand high temperatures, allowing for browning and crisping.

If you want to make a recipe in this book in another type of pan, you will need to adjust accordingly, and the results may vary. If you choose to use enameled cast iron, for instance, the pan should not be preheated without the addition of a fat, and you should be aware that enameled cast iron is only oven safe to a temperature of 500°F/260°C. To adjust the recipes, simply lower the temperatures and use additional fat.

HOW TO CARE FOR CAST IRON

How do you care for your seasoned cast-iron pan? The simple answer is: Use it, clean it (avoid abrasives), dry it, re-oil it occasionally, and use it again.

For the most part you only need to wipe out your pan, or use a small amount of coarse salt and a damp dish towel to rub away any debris. Using mild soap and water and not scrubbing too hard is fine, but only once in a while. Your pans always need to be dried thoroughly after washing to avoid rust.

What Not to Do

Cast iron is so easy to use, but there are things to avoid:

- Do not ever put cast iron in the dishwasher.

- Do not ever put cast iron in the microwave.

- Do not store food in cast iron.

- Do not freeze food in cast iron.

- Do not use utensils that will gouge the seasoning.

- Do not clean cast iron with copper or brass scrubbers.

- Avoid using cast iron to boil water because it will degrade your seasoned coating.

- Avoid simmering highly acidic foods, such as wine and tomatoes, for prolonged periods, unless the pan is well seasoned. Acids react with the iron, causing discoloration and off-tasting food. If you use too much acid, it can cause pitting, too.

- Cast iron may pick up flavors from time to time — fish in particular — so avoid baking or making vegetarian dishes in the same skillet used to cook meat dishes.

REVIVING A CAST-IRON PAN

Many times people will see a cast-iron pan that's rusty and think it's beyond repair. The truth is, as long as it isn't warped and doesn't have any cracks or major pitting, it can be brought back to life, with a little know-how.

The directions below are *only* to revive a rusted, scaled pan that needs to be reseasoned from scratch. Do not apply these methods to pans that aren't rusty. For those, just use lots of salt and elbow grease.

METHOD 1: Start by boiling some water in the cast-iron pan to lift up any basic grime or scaling. Next, use a scrubbing pad to clean off the rust and carbonization. If you have an orbital hand sander, try that, too. That should be all you need. Wash with hot soapy water before seasoning.

METHOD 2: If the first method doesn't work, your next option is (while wearing gloves and following the manufacturer's directions for use) to spray a light coating of oven cleaner that contains lye all over the pan, inside and out. Cover completely with plastic wrap and place in a paper bag, then in a rubber tub. Let the pan rest, somewhere warm, for up to 3 days. Lye is strong, so keep an eye on the tub and make sure the cleaner hasn't eaten through it.

After that time, and while wearing gloves, unwrap the pan in a well-ventilated area. The grime should be softened; if not, apply another coating of cleaner, and wait another day or so. When the oven cleaner has worked, use a scouring pad to scrub away the grime. When it's back to the original matte color, wash with hot soapy water, season again, and use!

METHOD 3: If you're interested in trying a more natural method, there is always molasses. Make a solution of 1 part molasses to 9 parts water, and soak the pan in the solution for 3 weeks in a warm place. As with lye, the molasses can eat through the container; keep an eye out for leaks. At the end of that time, the molasses may have fermented slightly. Don't worry. Rinse the pan off, give it a salt scrub, and all of the rust should be gone; then season as if it were new.

ABOUT SALT IN THE RECIPES

Salt types and amounts are not usually specified. You can use table or kosher salt for any of the recipes, unless specified. Just add salt to your taste. The exception to that rule is for baking. Always follow the amounts prescribed for baking, and use table salt. Kosher salt crystals are large, and the amount of salt in a tablespoon of kosher versus table salt can vary widely.

RECIPES

DUTCH BABY

with blueberry sauce

BEHOLD THE DUTCH BABY.
It's a delectable American version of a German popover that's ideal for an elegant breakfast. No bowls needed; just a blender, a pan, and a sieve for the powdered sugar. The lemon it is served with adds a welcome touch of acidity.

DUTCH BABY

4	tablespoons (½ stick) butter, cut into pieces
3	eggs, lightly beaten
1	cup whole milk
¾	cup all-purpose flour
1	tablespoon granulated sugar
1	teaspoon vanilla extract
	Pinch of ground nutmeg
	Pinch of salt
2	tablespoons confectioners' sugar
	Lemon wedges and blueberry sauce, for serving

BLUEBERRY SAUCE

2	pints blueberries, fresh or frozen
¼	cup granulated sugar
1	tablespoon lemon juice

   Serves 4–6

1   Scatter the butter into a 10-inch cast-iron skillet. Place on the middle rack of the oven and preheat to 450°F/230°C.

2   Meanwhile, pour the eggs into a blender and blend on high until light and foamy. Remove the lid and add the milk, flour, granulated sugar, vanilla, nutmeg, and salt. Blend again until all the ingredients are completely incorporated.

3   Remove the pan from the oven, pour in the batter, and return to the oven immediately. Bake for 15 to 20 minutes, or until golden and puffy.

4   While the Dutch baby cooks, make the blueberry sauce. In a nonreactive saucepan, stir together the blueberries, granulated sugar, and lemon juice. Simmer until the blueberries begin to pop, about 15 minutes. Mash lightly to release more juice. Let cool.

5   When the Dutch baby is done, remove from the oven and use an offset spatula to lift it onto a cutting board. Cut into wedges. Sift confectioners' sugar over each piece and serve with lemon wedges and blueberry sauce.

FULL ENGLISH

with bacon and sausages

THE FULL ENGLISH *is a classic weekend breakfast in England. It seems as if it has a lot of components, but they come together quickly and are mostly cooked in the same pan, and the bacon fat ties all the flavors together. For it to be spot on (and most classic), seek out English pork sausages called bangers or use pork and leek sausages.*

INGREDIENTS

8	strips bacon
4	pork sausages, preferably bangers
1	(16-ounce) can baked beans
1	cup halved button mushrooms
2	large tomatoes, cut into thick slices, or 4 Roma tomatoes, halved
2	tablespoons butter
8	slices bread
4	eggs
	Ketchup for serving (optional)

Serves 4

1   Put a platter in the oven, set to 200°F/90°C, or turned off if it is normally warm.

2   Add the bacon, in a single layer, to a 12-inch cast-iron skillet. Cook over medium heat, turning a few times until crispy, about 8 minutes. Remove and blot with paper towels. Remove the platter from the oven, put the bacon on the platter, cover with foil, and return the platter to the oven.

3   Cook the sausages in the bacon fat, turning frequently. This may take up to 10 minutes. When they're ready, remove and add to the platter in the oven.

4   While the sausages cook, heat the baked beans in a small saucepan over low heat.

5   Cook the mushrooms in the remaining fat, until browned, about 4 minutes. Transfer to the platter.

6   Add the tomatoes to the pan, cook until browned, about 2 minutes, then add to the platter in the oven.

7   In another 12-inch cast-iron skillet, over medium heat, melt the butter and fry the bread, cooking 3 minutes per side, adding more butter if needed. The bread should be quite browned and saturated.

8   Meanwhile, crack the eggs directly into the pan that held the tomatoes and cook until the yolks are set to your preference.

9   Divide all the components between four warmed plates. Serve with ketchup, if desired.

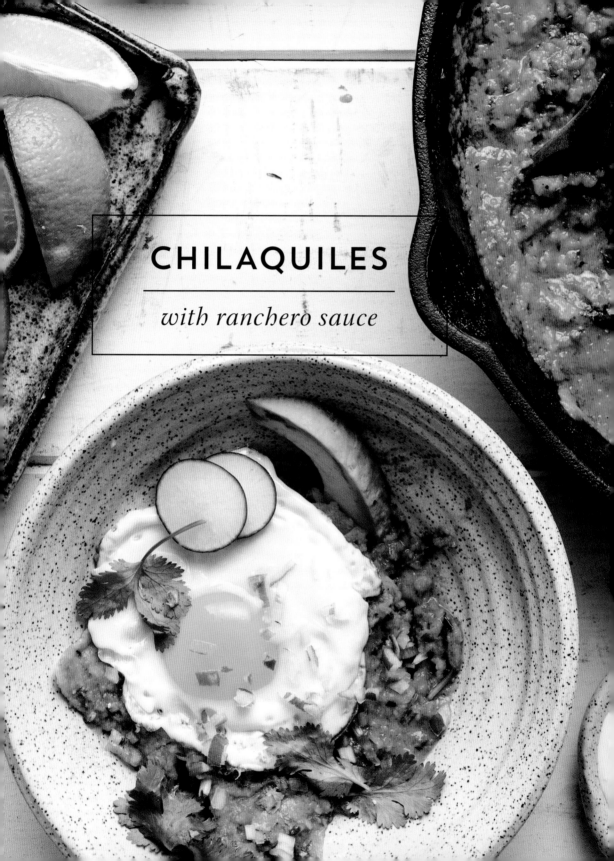

CHILAQUILES

with ranchero sauce

CHILAQUILES *is a bit of a "throw everything but the kitchen sink into the pan" sort of a meal, but it's a snap if your fridge is stocked with basic Latin ingredients. Think of it as breakfast nachos. This is also a great way to use up leftover grilled chicken or chorizo; add them as a garnish when serving.*

RANCHERO SAUCE

3	medium tomatoes, cored and halved
3	red jalapeño chiles, stemmed and seeded
1	red serrano chile, stemmed and seeded
2	garlic cloves, peeled
2	tablespoons vegetable oil
	Juice from 1 lime
	Salt

CHILAQUILES

¼	cup plus 2 teaspoons corn oil
1	cup water
¼	cup chopped fresh cilantro
3	cups tortilla chips
4	eggs
	Salt
1	red onion, chopped fine
6	radishes, sliced thin
1	avocado, sliced
½	cup Mexican crema or sour cream
¼	cup crumbled Cotija cheese
	Lime wedges and hot sauce, for serving

1   To make the ranchero sauce, place a 12-inch cast-iron skillet over high heat. Add the tomatoes, jalapeños, serrano, and garlic, and char until slightly blackened, about 3 minutes. Scoop the vegetables into a blender, add the vegetable oil and lime juice, and purée until smooth. Pour into a bowl and season with salt. Taste and adjust seasoning as needed. Set aside. The sauce can be refrigerated for up to 1 week.

2   For the chilaquiles, add ¼ cup of the corn oil to a 12-inch cast-iron skillet over medium heat. Carefully add the ranchero sauce and water to the pan and bring to a simmer. Stir in the cilantro, remove from the heat, toss in 2 cups of the tortilla chips, cover, and let rest. You want the tortilla chips to absorb the sauce.

3   In another skillet, heat the remaining 2 teaspoons corn oil over medium heat. Crack the eggs directly into the pan and cook until the whites are set, about 3 minutes. Using a spatula, transfer the eggs to a plate, making sure not to break the yolks.

4   Uncover the tortilla chip mixture and return to the stove, over low heat. Simmer and season to taste with salt if necessary.

5   Divide the chip mixture among four shallow bowls and top with a fried egg.

6   Top with the red onion, radishes, avocado, crema, and cheese. Serve with the remaining 1 cup tortilla chips, lime wedges, and hot sauce.

BREAKFAST POTATOES

the classic favorite

THESE BREAKFAST POTATOES
are the undressed version of the classic breakfast dish. They go with everything from pancakes to scrambled eggs. Additions could include diced red onion, celery, and bell pepper. You can make these ahead of time and even freeze them for up to 2 months; just defrost, if needed, and reheat in a well-oiled pan.

INGREDIENTS

4   baking potatoes, cut into bite-size pieces

Salt

3   tablespoons vegetable oil

1   tablespoon ground sweet or smoked
      paprika

Large pinch of ground cayenne pepper

Freshly ground black pepper

Serves 4–6

1   Preheat the oven to 400°F/200°C.

2   Place the potatoes and a generous pinch of salt in a large pot and add enough water to cover. Bring to a boil and let cook for 5 minutes, until the potatoes are just parcooked, then drain them.

3   Place the potatoes in a bowl and toss with 2 tablespoons of the oil, along with the paprika, cayenne, and salt and pepper to taste.

4   Heat the remaining 1 tablespoon oil in a 12-inch cast-iron skillet over medium-high heat for 1 minute. Add the potatoes to the pan in a single layer. Let brown for 5 to 6 minutes, without stirring. Then turn the potatoes.

5   Place the pan in the oven and roast for 20 to 30 minutes, until the potatoes are golden brown and crisp, turning once.

GRILLED CHEESE

extra-golden and delicious

GRILLED CHEESE, *with its two slices of bread binding ooey-gooey cheese, is perfectly suited to the dark black surface of a cast-iron pan. The light coating of mayo on the outside of the bread makes the sandwiches extragolden. Serve with tomato soup.*

INGREDIENTS

8   slices cheese, preferably American or a combination of American and cheddar

8   slices top-quality white sandwich bread

    Mayonnaise

8   teaspoons butter, softened (plus more as needed)

    Salt

Makes 4 sandwiches

1   Heat a 12-inch cast-iron skillet over medium-high heat (or, if cooking outdoors, over a low campfire or on the cooler side of a grill).

2   Meanwhile, build the four sandwiches. Arrange two slices of cheese on each bottom slice of bread and top with the other slice of bread. Carefully spread mayonnaise on the top slice.

3   When the pan is hot, add 2 teaspoons of the butter and a nice sprinkle of salt and lower the heat to medium.

4   Add the first sandwich, mayo-covered slice down. Press down with a spatula and let cook for 3 minutes, or until golden.

5   Remove the sandwich from the pan and carefully spread more mayo on the top of the uncooked slice of bread. Flip and return the sandwich to the pan. Press and cook until golden brown, adding more butter as needed.

6   Remove the sandwich from the pan and set aside while you cook the remaining sandwiches, adding 2 teaspoons of the butter and salt to the pan each time. Cut each sandwich on the diagonal and serve immediately.

FRENCH TOMATO SOUP

with fennel and orange

FRENCH TOMATO SOUP, *with its acidic tomatoes, can pick up a metallic taste when cooked in seasoned cast iron. To avoid that, this soup is started in a cast-iron pan, then transferred to a blender (or, use an enameled cast-iron pan and skip the blender).*

INGREDIENTS

3   tablespoons unsalted butter

1   small baguette, torn into bite-size pieces

Salt

1   onion, peeled and quartered

1   fennel bulb, cored and roughly chopped, fronds reserved for garnish

2   carrots, peeled and chopped

2   garlic cloves, peeled

1   teaspoon minced fresh thyme

3   cups vegetable broth

2   tablespoons butter

Juice and zest of 1 small orange

4   small tomatoes, cored and roughly chopped

1   (28-ounce) can crushed tomatoes

Freshly ground black pepper

 *Makes four 1-cup servings*

1   Arrange a wire rack over a baking sheet.

2   Melt the unsalted butter in a large Dutch oven over medium-high heat. Add the torn bread and cook until browned, turning frequently. Remove with a slotted spoon and season immediately with salt. Reserve until the soup is ready.

3   Wipe out the Dutch oven, leaving a bit of oil behind, and set aside.

4   In a food processor, coarsely chop the onion, fennel, carrots, and garlic.

5   Heat the Dutch oven over medium-high heat, add the onion mixture and thyme, and cook until soft, about 6 minutes, stirring frequently. Add the broth and butter and bring to a simmer.

6   Wipe out the work bowl of the food processor and carefully ladle the mixture back into it. Add the orange juice and half of the orange zest, rough-chopped tomatoes, and crushed tomatoes. Process until smooth. Season with salt and pepper to taste.

7   Serve garnished with a few croutons, fennel fronds, and the remaining orange zest.

CHEESY FONDUE

with beer

CHEESY FONDUE *is perfect for cheese lovers. Melted cheese is great in any form: pizza, grilled cheese, quesadillas — you name it. This fondue simply enables you to take that love to a new level. If you're like me, this is the recipe for you. This also works great over a low campfire, but use a Dutch oven and double the ingredients.*

INGREDIENTS

1 garlic clove

2 cups grated cheese, (try a mix of Swiss, cheddar, Monterey Jack, and Havarti)

2 teaspoons cornstarch

1 teaspoon Colman's mustard powder

2 cups pale ale

Chopped fresh parsley, for garnish

Bread cubes and assorted vegetables, for serving

 Serves 4–6

1 Rub the bottom of a 10-inch cast-iron skillet with the garlic clove and set aside.

2 In a bowl, toss the grated cheese with the cornstarch and mustard powder to coat.

3 Heat the garlic-rubbed skillet over low heat, add the beer, and bring to a simmer. Whisk in the cheese in four parts, letting the cheese melt completely before adding more.

4 Serve while still warm and bubbling, garnished with parsley and with a plate of bread and assorted vegetables on the side.

PAN PIZZA

choose your toppings

PAN PIZZA *is everything good about the toppings on a regular pie, with the addition of lots and lots of baked crust. The recipe makes enough dough for two pies. If you're only making one pie, store the extra dough in a covered bowl or container in the refrigerator for up to 2 days. Bring to room temperature before using.*

INGREDIENTS

2½	cups plus 2 tablespoons warm water
1	teaspoon molasses
1	packet (2¼ teaspoons) active dry yeast
5	cups all-purpose flour
¼	cup olive oil, plus 2 teaspoons to drizzle on top
2	tablespoons yellow cornmeal
1	cup tomato sauce (or pizza sauce)
1½	cups assorted grated cheese, including mozzarella and provolone
½	cup freshly grated Parmesan cheese
	Assorted pizza toppings

1 Whisk together 2 tablespoons of the warm water and the molasses in a medium bowl. Sprinkle the yeast on top and let rest for 2 minutes, until it becomes foamy.

2 Meanwhile, add the flour to the bowl of a stand mixer fitted with a dough hook. With the mixer running at low speed, slowly add the yeasted water and one-third of the remaining 2½ cups warm water. Add ¼ cup of the oil, then add another third of the water. Continue adding water until the dough comes together and is a smooth ball. This will take about 8 minutes.

3 Place the dough in a lightly oiled bowl, cover with a clean cloth, and let rise for 1 hour.

4 Preheat the oven to 450°F/230°C. Oil the bottom and sides of a 12-inch cast-iron skillet.

5 Punch down the dough and divide it in half. Stretch one half of the dough into a wide circle. Sprinkle a 12-inch cast-iron skillet with 1 tablespoon of the cornmeal and place the dough in the skillet, cover, and let rise for 15 minutes. Do the same with the remaining dough in a second skillet, or reserve that dough for later.

6 Shape the dough in the skillet again, making sure it is thicker on the edges, by pressing the center.

7 Parbake the crust for 10 minutes. Remove from the oven and allow to cool slightly. Add the sauce, cheeses, and toppings, then drizzle with the remaining 2 teaspoons oil and return to the oven.

8 Bake for 25 minutes, or until the sauce is bubbly and the toppings are golden brown.

LUNCH & DINNER

SPANAKOPITA

with pine nuts

THIS SPANAKOPITA *is my variation on the classic Greek dish, with the addition of pine nuts and some sun-dried tomatoes. A cast-iron pan helps crisp the phyllo in a way most other pans can't. In this recipe the spinach doesn't actually touch the sides of the pan, so the spinach won't discolor or react in any way.*

INGREDIENTS

3	cups frozen spinach, defrosted and coarsely chopped
2	eggs, lightly beaten
¼	cup pine nuts or walnuts, toasted and coarsely chopped
¼	cup minced sun-dried tomatoes
2	cups crumbled feta cheese
½	cup grated Parmigiano-Reggiano cheese
½	cup minced fresh dill
¼	teaspoon ground nutmeg
	Freshly ground black pepper
⅓	cup olive oil
1	package phyllo dough sheets, thawed in the refrigerator

Serves 6

1 Preheat the oven to 375°F/190°C.

2 Squeeze out any excess moisture from the spinach.

3 In a large bowl, combine the eggs, pine nuts, sun-dried tomatoes, feta, Parmigiano-Reggiano, dill, and nutmeg. Stir to combine. Stir in the spinach and season generously with pepper.

4 Using a pastry brush and working quickly, lightly oil one side of a phyllo sheet and lay it, oiled side down, in a 10-inch skillet so it comes up the sides. Repeat with three more sheets of phyllo, making sure to lay them in different directions and leaving quite a bit of overhang.

5 Spread the filling on the phyllo. Top with three more sheets of phyllo that have been trimmed to fit the skillet. Fold the overhanging phyllo on top, and brush with additional oil.

6 Using a sharp knife, score the phyllo into six wedges.

7 Bake the spanakopita for 35 to 45 minutes, or until the top crust is golden brown. Let cool until just warm. Cut along the score marks to serve.

MUSHROOMS & TOFU

over rice

MUSHROOMS & TOFU *is a family creation. When my twin niece and nephew were 3 years old, they started asking to help in the kitchen. There were lots of funny mishaps, but out of those mistakes came this recipe. This dish will work as a vegetarian entrée or as a side dish.*

INGREDIENTS

¼   cup vegetable oil

2   cups halved mushrooms

2   cups cubed extra-firm tofu

2   heaping tablespoons cornstarch

½   onion, minced

¼   cup soy sauce

2   tablespoons water

Steamed rice, for serving

Serves 4–6

1   Add the oil to a 12-inch cast-iron skillet and heat over medium heat. Carefully arrange the mushrooms in the hot oil, cut side down. Let the mushrooms brown for a few minutes without stirring.

2   Meanwhile, pat the tofu dry and toss with the cornstarch. Add the tofu and onion to the mushrooms and let cook until golden.

3   Add the soy sauce and water. Reduce the heat and let simmer for 2 minutes. Serve with steamed rice.

TZIMMES

with seitan

TZIMMES *is a sweet-and-savory vegetable stew that's typically served in the fall as part of the Jewish holidays. It's warming and redolent of autumn flavors. Here, to make it a complete, hearty meal, I've added seitan (a meat substitute made of gluten). Serve this stew with corn bread, brown rice, or buttered noodles.*

INGREDIENTS

1	tablespoon olive oil
1	onion, in large dice
2	cups seitan cubes
2	large sweet potatoes, peeled, in large dice
4	large carrots, peeled, in large dice
1	large apple, peeled and cored, in large dice
½	cup dried apricots, halved
1	cup dried plums, pitted (optional)
2	teaspoons salt
1	teaspoon brown sugar
	Small pinch of ground cinnamon
	Zest and juice of 1 large orange
1	cup apple juice

Serves 4–6

1   In a 5-quart Dutch oven, heat the oil over medium-high heat. Add the onion and seitan and sauté until slightly browned, about 5 minutes.

2   Add the sweet potatoes, carrots, apple, apricots, dried plums (if using), salt, sugar, cinnamon, orange zest and juice, and apple juice to the pan. Bring to a simmer, uncovered, and cook for about 15 minutes, or until the vegetables soften.

3   Taste and adjust the seasonings. Remove from the heat and serve.

VEGETARIAN THREE-BEAN FIREHOUSE CHILI

great for a crowd

VEGETARIAN THREE-BEAN FIREHOUSE CHILI *should only be made in a well-seasoned cast-iron or enameled Dutch oven. If your seasoning isn't well established, the tomato can discolor and take up a metallic taste. Serve with corn bread or over pasta.*

INGREDIENTS

2	teaspoons olive oil
1	large onion, chopped
3	stalks celery, chopped
2	carrots, peeled and chopped
1	red bell pepper, chopped
1	cup chopped mushrooms
1	jalapeño pepper, seeded and finely chopped
1	pasilla pepper, seeded and finely chopped
1	Anaheim pepper, seeded and finely chopped
2	tablespoons tomato paste
4	garlic cloves, finely chopped
¼	cup chili powder
1	teaspoon dried oregano
½	teaspoon ground cumin
3	cups water
1	(28-ounce) can crushed tomatoes
1	cup TVP (optional; see note)
1	cup cooked kidney beans
1	cup cooked black beans
1	cup cooked pinto beans
	Salt
	Grated cheese, diced onion, and sour cream, for serving

Serves 8–10

1   Heat the oil in a large cast-iron Dutch oven over medium heat.

2   Add the onion, celery, carrots, bell pepper, mushrooms, and chiles, and cook, stirring occasionally, for 5 minutes, or until lightly browned.

3   Stir in the tomato paste, garlic, chili powder, oregano, and cumin, and cook for another 3 minutes.

4   Add the water, crushed tomatoes, TVP (if using), kidney beans, black beans, pinto beans, and salt to taste.

5   Simmer for 25 minutes. Taste and adjust the seasoning as needed. Serve topped with grated cheese, diced onion, and sour cream. Any extra can be frozen for up to 6 months.

Note: *TVP stands for texturized vegetable protein. TVP looks like ground meat but is made completely from vegetable protein. It rehydrates when added to wet ingredients. It will make the stew really hearty (and still vegetarian).*

MANGO CURRY

with cashews

THIS MANGO CURRY *is an Indian-style vegetarian dish. Without the yogurt, it's also completely vegan. Look for mangoes that are slightly soft, so they have that wonderful fruity-spicy flavor. They will brown and release a bit of juice that adds something mysterious and beautiful to the finished dish.*

 Serves 4–6

INGREDIENTS

4	mangoes
3	tablespoons coconut oil
½	cup cashew pieces
1	teaspoon ground cayenne pepper
1	teaspoon ground turmeric
½	teaspoon brown mustard seeds
1	teaspoon brown sugar
1	cup water
2	serrano chiles, sliced
1	garlic clove, sliced
½	teaspoon cumin seeds
	Salt
	Rice and plain yogurt, for serving

1   Dice the mangoes and reserve ½ cup for garnish.

2   In a 12-inch cast-iron skillet, heat 2 tablespoons of the oil over high heat. Add the mangoes and cook until some of the liquid is released and the mangoes brown slightly, about 3 minutes. Stir sparingly.

3   Add the cashew pieces, cayenne, tumeric, and mustard seeds, and stir to coat. After 30 seconds, add the sugar and water (more if the mangoes were very dry).

4   Lower the heat and let simmer for 10 minutes, mashing the mango pieces with a spoon as they cook. When the mangoes are cooked down, taste and adjust the seasoning as needed.

5   In a 10-inch cast-iron skillet, heat the remaining 1 tablespoon oil over medium-high heat and quickly fry the chiles, garlic, cumin seeds, and salt to taste. After about 1 minute, remove from the heat and pour over the mango mixture.

6   Serve with rice and garnish with plain yogurt.

CLAM & CORN FRITTERS

with tarragon

CLAM & CORN FRITTERS *is a perfect summer dish that you can make year-round. You can shuck fresh clams or use canned — either way is fine. The fritters are similar to hush puppies, but with a briny aftertaste. Eat paired with a crisp rosé, preferably outdoors.*

INGREDIENTS

48	cherrystone clams or 2 cups canned clam meat
4	ears corn
1	cup fine cornmeal
1	cup all-purpose flour
2	teaspoons baking powder
	Salt and freshly ground black pepper
2	egg yolks, gently beaten
½	cup coarsely chopped fresh tarragon, or other fresh herbs
2	egg whites
4	cups vegetable oil
	Hot sauce, for serving

1 Arrange a wire rack on top of a baking sheet.

2 If you are using fresh clams, shuck them over a bowl, then strain and save the liquid. Coarsely chop the clam meat.

3 Cut the kernels from the corncobs.

4 In another bowl, combine the cornmeal and flour. Add the baking powder and salt and pepper to taste and stir well. Add the egg yolks and stir. Add the clams, corn, and tarragon and blend well. The batter should be stiff, but add the reserved clam juice if it seems too dry.

5 Using a hand mixer or a whisk, beat the egg whites until soft peaks hold.

6 Gently fold the egg whites into the clam mixture in three parts. Do not overmix.

7 Heat 2 cups of the oil in a 12-inch cast-iron skillet over medium-high heat until the temperature of the oil is 350°F/175°C. Carefully drop in teaspoons of the batter, making sure not to crowd the fritters. (They will expand.) They should float after about 10 seconds in the oil; stir gently so they don't settle on the bottom of the pan.

8 Cook until browned, turning as needed. As the fritters are cooked, transfer to the wire rack and salt immediately. Add more oil as needed and keep the temperature around 350°F/175°C.

9 When all of the fritters are done, serve with hot sauce.

LUNCH & DINNER

SALMON CAKES

with tartar sauce

SALMON CAKES *are a clever way to use leftover salmon from last night's dinner. You can also poach some fresh fish or use canned. It's up to you. The Worcestershire sauce adds a bit of umami, the mayo keeps everything moist, and the dill gives it a little perk.*

SALMON CAKES

2	cups flaked cooked salmon
1⅔	cups panko breadcrumbs (plus more if needed)
1	egg, lightly beaten
2	tablespoons mayonnaise
1	tablespoon minced fresh dill
2	teaspoons capers, chopped
1	teaspoon Worcestershire sauce
	Salt and freshly ground black pepper
3	tablespoons vegetable oil
	Lemon wedges, for serving

TARTAR SAUCE

¾	cup mayonnaise
2	tablespoons lemon juice
2	gherkin pickles, finely chopped
1	tablespoon capers, finely chopped

Serves 4–6, or makes 24 appetizer bites

1 In a large bowl, combine the salmon and ⅔ cup of the breadcrumbs.

2 Add the egg, mayonnaise, dill, capers, Worcestershire, and salt and pepper to taste, mixing well. Form into patties (4 inches wide for entrées or 1½ inches wide for appetizers).

3 Place the remaining 1 cup breadcrumbs on a wide, shallow plate. Gently coat each salmon patty in the breadcrumbs, shaking off any excess. Place the coated patties on a plate while you coat the remaining patties.

4 In a 12-inch cast-iron skillet, heat the oil over medium-high heat. Add half the salmon cakes in a single layer. Cook 3 minutes per side, until golden brown. Transfer the cooked patties to a paper towel–lined plate.

5 To make the tartar sauce, combine the mayonnaise, lemon juice, pickles, and capers in a large bowl and mix well. If not using immediately, cover and refrigerate for up to 5 days.

6 Serve the salmon cakes with lemon wedges and tartar sauce.

BAKED CRAB & SHRIMP

with fish stock

BAKED CRAB AND SHRIMP *is an étouffée-style crab dish that starts with the holy trinity of Cajun cooking — celery, onion, and green bell pepper. If you don't have fish stock available, use clam juice. Serve this with rice, corn bread, or a side dish of baked onions.*

INGREDIENTS

4	tablespoons (½ stick) butter
2	stalks celery, minced
1	onion, minced
1	green bell pepper, minced
2	garlic cloves, minced
	Large pinch of ground cayenne pepper
	Large pinch of chili powder
2	teaspoons all-purpose flour
1½	cups fish stock
1½	cups lump crabmeat
1	pound shrimp, peeled and deveined
¼	cup heavy cream
1	cup breadcrumbs
1	bunch scallions, sliced thin
	Rice, corn bread, or baked onions, for serving

1   Preheat the broiler.

2   Melt the butter in a 10-inch cast-iron pan over medium heat.

3   Add the celery, onion, bell pepper, garlic, cayenne, and chili powder. Cook, stirring frequently, until the vegetables are soft. Do not let the vegetables brown. Sprinkle the vegetables evenly with the flour and continue to cook for another 2 minutes, stirring constantly.

4   Slowly add the stock. Bring to a simmer, reduce the heat, and cook until slightly thickened, 6 to 8 minutes.

5   Add the crab, shrimp, and cream to the vegetables and raise the heat slightly. Cook until the shrimp has turned pink, about 2 minutes.

6   Meanwhile, combine the breadcrumbs and scallions in a small bowl. Scatter over the skillet mixture.

7   Place the skillet under the broiler and cook until the breadcrumbs are lightly browned. Serve family-style.

MUSSELS

with white wine

MUSSELS WITH WHITE WINE

is my favorite meal to serve to guests. Other than some chopping, there's nothing to it; the ingredients are inexpensive, and the results are sublime. A piled-high bowl of mussels in a luscious, flavorful broth is a thing of beauty. Serve with a large slice of garlicky toasted bread or a heaping pile of salty French fries.

AIOLI

¾   cup mayonnaise

2   garlic cloves, mashed to paste

¼   cup finely minced fresh tarragon
     Salt

MUSSELS

4   pounds mussels (see note)

4   tablespoons butter

6   garlic cloves, finely chopped

2   shallots, chopped

2   stalks celery, chopped

1   bulb fennel, chopped (reserve the
     fronds for garnish)

2   cups dry white wine

2   tablespoons chopped fresh tarragon
     Toasted bread or French fries, for serving

Serves 4 as an entrée

1   To make the aioli, combine the mayonnaise, garlic, and tarragon in a small bowl and mix well. Season with salt to taste and set aside.

2   Rinse the mussels well under cold water. Pick them over, pulling off any beards and discarding any that are cracked.

3   In a large cast-iron Dutch oven, melt 2 tablespoons of the butter over medium-high heat. Add the garlic, shallots, celery, and fennel, and cook until soft but not colored, stirring often, about 3 minutes.

4   Add the mussels, wine, and tarragon. Immediately cover the pan and increase the heat to high. Cook for 3 minutes, shaking the pan once or twice.

5   Remove the lid, add the remaining 2 tablespoons butter, and stir. Cover and cook for 3 minutes longer, again shaking the pan once or twice.

6   To serve, divide the mussels and broth among warmed bowls. Garnish with aioli and chopped fennel fronds. Serve with toasted bread or French fries to sop up the broth.

Note: *When you buy mussels, ask the fishmonger to clean them. It will save you a bit of time and struggle trying to remove the inedible beards they sometimes come with.*

PAN-SEARED, PECAN-CRUSTED FISH

with fried green tomatoes

LUNCH & DINNER

PAN-SEARED, PECAN-CRUSTED FISH *can be cooked outside; just be sure to place the pan on a grate over a low fire and follow the directions from there. Serve with roasted potatoes or spaghetti squash. You can't go wrong either way.*

INGREDIENTS

1	cup all-purpose flour
1	cup milk
2	eggs
1	cup pecans, finely ground
1	cup fresh breadcrumbs
2	cups vegetable oil, for frying
4	(6-ounce) skinless fish fillets or 4 small, whole cleaned trout
4	green tomatoes, sliced

Serves 4

1 Prepare three shallow bowls: one with the flour, one with the milk and eggs whisked together, and one with a mixture of the pecans and breadcrumbs.

2 Heat the oil very slowly in a deep 12-inch cast-iron skillet to 350°F/175°C.

3 Dredge the fish in the flour, then the milk and egg mixture, then the pecan and breadcrumb mixture. Shake off any excess.

4 Fry the fish for 2 minutes per side, until golden brown. Drain on a paper towel–lined plate.

5 Repeat steps 3 and 4 with the green tomatoes and serve with the fish.

TURKEY PICCATA

with capers

THIS TURKEY PICCATA *contains capers, the edible flower buds of a shrubby plant that grows in dry climates. They are pickled and brined and used as a seasoning. It is a good idea to rinse them before using, to remove excess brine that may be overly salty.*

INGREDIENTS

¼   cup all-purpose flour

     Salt and freshly ground black pepper

6–8 thin turkey cutlets

2   tablespoons olive oil

3   tablespoons butter

1   cup white wine

     Juice of 1 lemon

2   tablespoons capers, rinsed

1   tablespoon chopped fresh parsley

 Serves 4–6

1   On a wide, shallow plate, combine the flour with salt and pepper to taste.

2   Dredge each turkey cutlet in the seasoned flour, turning to coat thoroughly. Shake off any excess.

3   Heat the oil and 1 tablespoon of the butter in a 10-inch cast-iron skillet over medium-high heat.

4   Arrange the turkey cutlets in the pan; avoid crowding them. Cook until browned, 2 to 3 minutes for each side.

5   Transfer the turkey to a platter. Pour out any excess fat from the skillet.

6   Add the wine and the remaining 2 tablespoons butter to the skillet. Cook until the liquid is reduced by half, about 1 minute. Whisk in the lemon juice and capers. Pour the sauce over the turkey, garnish with parsley, and serve.

BRICK CHICKEN

with sage

FOR BRICK CHICKEN, *you will need one or two bricks, wrapped in foil. You can also use another, smaller cast-iron skillet, weighed down with something heatproof. (Do not use cans of food as weights; they will get hot.) This is all about even cooking and really crispy skin.*

INGREDIENTS

½   cup (1 stick) butter, at room temperature

2   tablespoons finely chopped fresh sage

1   tablespoon finely chopped fresh rosemary

1   lemon, zested and quartered

1   small chicken, no more than 3½ pounds

   Salt and freshly ground black pepper

   Lemon wedges, for serving

Serves 4–6

1   Preheat the oven to 375°F/190°C.

2   In a small bowl, combine all but 2 tablespoons of the softened butter with the sage, rosemary, and lemon zest.

3   Using heavy kitchen shears, cut the backbone out of the chicken (or have your butcher do this). Flip the chicken over, then gently push down until it flattens, opening like a book.

4   Working gently, loosen the skin on the chicken (leaving it attached) and ease the seasoned butter in between the skin and the breast. Massage to distribute evenly. Pat the chicken dry, coat with the remaining 2 tablespoons butter, and salt and pepper liberally on all sides.

5   Heat a 12-inch cast-iron skillet over medium-high heat. Carefully lay the chicken, skin side down, in the skillet and weigh it down with foil-wrapped bricks. Reduce the heat to medium-low and cook for about 20 minutes.

6   With a metal spatula, carefully flip the chicken over so that it's skin side up. Add the quartered lemons to the pan and roast in the oven for 15 to 20 minutes, until the thigh reaches 165°F/75°C.

7   Carve as desired. Serve with the pan juices and lemon wedges.

FRIED CHICKEN

with spices

FRIED CHICKEN *can probably be made in millions of ways, each with its own proponent. This version is designed to give maximum flavor and lots of crispy coating. Soaking the chicken in buttermilk and spices ahead of time adds another layer of flavor and keeps the chicken moist.*

INGREDIENTS

2	tablespoons ground paprika
2	teaspoons freshly ground black pepper
1	teaspoon ground cayenne pepper
¼	cup salt
2	quarts buttermilk
4	pounds assorted chicken pieces
4	cups all-purpose flour
2	eggs, lightly beaten
1	tablespoon cornstarch
3	cups vegetable shortening or vegetable oil (or lard)

 Serves 4–6

1 In a small bowl, stir together the paprika, black pepper, and cayenne.

2 Four to six hours before you want to fry the chicken, combine the salt and half of the spice mix in a large container. (Reserve the rest of the spice mix for step 4.) Add all but 1 cup of the buttermilk and stir to combine. Add the chicken pieces, cover, and refrigerate.

3 Remove the chicken from the refrigerator 30 to 40 minutes prior to frying. Drain the chicken in a colander. Discard the buttermilk.

4 Measure 1 cup of the flour into a shallow dish. In another larger dish, whisk together the eggs, the remaining 1 cup buttermilk, and the remaining spice mix. In a third dish, combine the remaining 3 cups flour and the cornstarch.

5 Meanwhile, heat the shortening to 425°F/ 220°C over medium-high heat in a 12-inch cast-iron skillet. Place a wire rack over a baking sheet.

6 Dredge each piece of chicken first in the plain flour, shaking off any excess. Next, dip in the buttermilk. Remove from the buttermilk and coat heavily in the flour and cornstarch mix.

7 Carefully arrange half of the chicken pieces skin side down in the pan and fry, turning twice, until deep golden brown on all sides and an instant-read thermometer reads 150°F/65°C for white meat and 165°F/75°C for dark meat, 8 to 10 minutes. Continue to monitor the oil temperature, which should stay at 425°F/220°C. Place the cooked chicken on the wire rack and let cool before serving.

KOREAN FRIED CHICKEN

with garlic and ginger

KOREAN FRIED CHICKEN, *or, as it's usually called, KFC, is magically delicious. You can play around with the amounts of garlic and ginger to make it perfect for your taste.*

INGREDIENTS

8–10	chicken thighs
2	teaspoons salt
5	garlic cloves, minced
1	(1-inch) piece fresh ginger, minced
¼	cup soy sauce
1	tablespoon sugar
⅓	cup *sambal oelek,* or to taste
2	tablespoons rice vinegar
1	teaspoon toasted sesame oil
	Peanut oil for frying
1	cup all-purpose flour
½	cup cornstarch
⅔	cup cold water

Note: *Sambal oelek (Asian chili paste) can be found in the Asian section of most markets.*

1   Toss the chicken thighs with the salt and let rest for 30 minutes.

2   To make the sauce, whisk together the minced garlic and ginger, soy sauce, sugar, sambal oelek, vinegar, and sesame oil in a medium bowl. Taste and adjust the seasoning as needed. Set aside.

3   Meanwhile, pour peanut oil into a 12-inch cast-iron pan, to 2 inches deep. Heat slowly over medium heat until it reaches 355°F/180°C. Arrange a wire rack on top of a baking sheet.

4   To make the batter, whisk together the flour, cornstarch, and cold water in a deep bowl.

5   Working in three batches, dip the chicken thighs in the batter, let the excess drip off, and add to the hot oil. Fry, using tongs to turn the chicken as needed, until the chicken is golden, 6 to 8 minutes total. When done, place on the wire rack to cool.

6   When all the chicken is fried, toss in the sauce and serve.

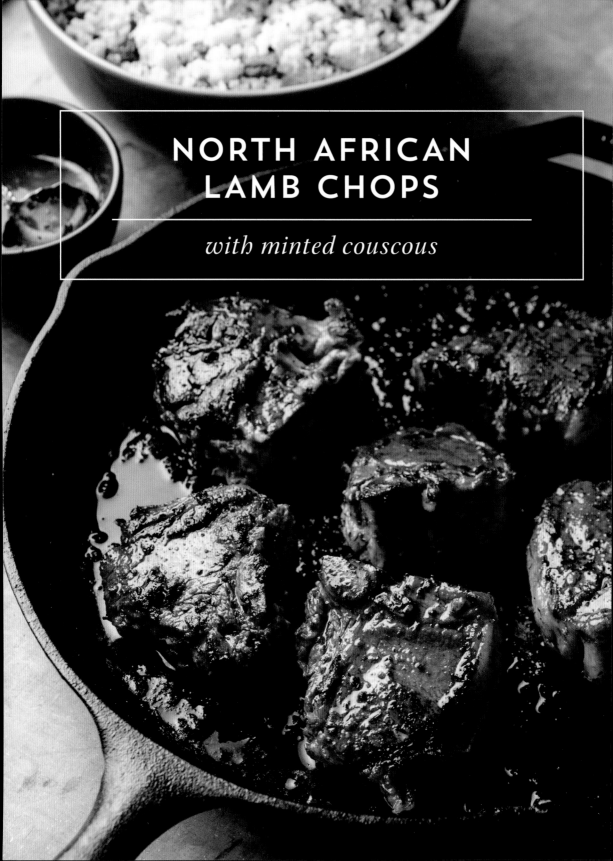

NORTH AFRICAN
LAMB CHOPS

with minted couscous

NORTH AFRICAN LAMB CHOPS *is made special by the* chermoula, *a North African herb sauce that can be made a day ahead. The addition of preserved lemons is lovely, but if you don't have any on hand, they can be omitted.*

LAMB

6   bone-in lamb loin chops
    Salt

CHERMOULA

1   cup fresh cilantro

1   cup fresh parsley

4   garlic cloves, chopped

1   teaspoon ground cumin

1   teaspoon ground paprika

1   teaspoon dried thyme
    Pinch of ground turmeric

1   tablespoon chopped preserved lemon peel

1   cup olive oil

½   cup lemon juice

1   large pinch of red pepper flakes
    Salt and freshly ground black pepper

COUSCOUS

2   cups water

1⅓ cups uncooked couscous

1   tablespoon dried mint

1   teaspoon salt
    Zest and juice of 1 lemon

1   cup chopped fresh mint

1   Season the lamb chops with salt and place in a shallow dish.

2   To make the chermoula, combine the cilantro, parsley, garlic, cumin, paprika, thyme, turmeric, lemon peel, oil, lemon juice, and pepper flakes in a food processor and process until smooth. Season to taste with salt and pepper.

3   Pour three-quarters of the chermoula over the lamb and rub in. Cover and let marinate for up to 10 hours in the refrigerator. Store the remaining chermoula in the refrigerator (bring to room temperature before serving).

4   To make the couscous, bring the water to a boil in a small saucepan. Add the couscous, dried mint, and salt. Cover and turn off the heat. Let steam for 8 minutes. Remove the lid and fluff the couscous with a fork. When slightly cooled, fold in the lemon zest and juice and the fresh mint, reserving some mint for garnish.

5   Heat a 12-inch cast-iron skillet over medium-high heat. Remove the chops from the marinade, wiping off any excess. Arrange half of the chops in the pan in a single layer, taking care not to crowd them. Cook until well browned on both sides, turning as needed, about 8 minutes total. Repeat with the other half of the chops.

6   Let the chops rest for 5 minutes before serving with the minted couscous and the remaining chermoula, garnished with the reserved fresh mint.

SAUSAGE & KALE

with lentils

SAUSAGE AND KALE, *paired with lentils, is a hearty dish. Crushing the kale a little with your hands softens it and makes the texture more manageable. Leftovers can be chopped up and added to a rich chicken stock for a filling soup. This dish can also be made outdoors on a grate over a medium-high fire.*

INGREDIENTS

4   cups dried brown lentils

6   cups plus 1 tablespoon water

    Salt

1   tablespoon olive oil

4   uncooked garlic sausages,
        split lengthwise

1   bunch kale, roughly chopped

5   garlic cloves, chopped

    Salt and freshly ground black pepper

Serves 4–6

1   Combine the lentils, 6 cups of water, and salt to taste in a small saucepan. Bring to a boil over high heat, then reduce to a simmer over medium-low and cook until lentils are tender, about 30 minutes. Drain and set aside.

2   Heat a 12-inch cast-iron skillet over medium-high heat and add the oil. Add the sausages and roast, turning once, until browned and cooked through, 15 to 20 minutes.

3   Meanwhile, using your hands, crush the kale until it's limp.

4   When the sausage is cooked, add the crushed kale and garlic. Sauté, turning often, for 2 minutes.

5   Add the remaining 1 tablespoon water, season to taste with salt and pepper, and cover. Let cook for 2 minutes, then uncover and add the lentils. Continue to cook, covered, until the lentils are warmed through, about 3 minutes.

GO-TO BURGERS

the perfect patties

THE KEY TO THESE GO-TO BURGERS *is the meat you put into the loosely formed patties. Have your butcher grind the meat for you, and you'll see and taste the difference. Ask for a mix of 70 percent chuck and 30 percent short rib meat. If you are feeling especially sinful, have them throw a few slices of bacon into the grind. This recipe works beautifully over a low campfire, too.*

INGREDIENTS

1¼   pounds ground beef

       Salt

1   tablespoon milk or water

       Toasted buns, tomato, lettuce, onion, and condiments, for serving

    Serves 4

1   Gently mix the beef with 1 teaspoon of salt and the milk. Form into four loose patties.

2   Heat a 12-inch cast-iron skillet over medium-high heat. Sprinkle some salt in the pan and add the burgers. Cook, without moving them, for 3 minutes. Flip and continue cooking for 4 minutes longer, or until they reach the desired doneness.

3   Let rest for 5 minutes before adding to a toasted bun, topping with condiments, and serving.

STEAKS

with red wine sauce

STEAKS *should be done right — don't skimp. Go to the butcher and ask for the best rib eye he or she has. Then go to the wine shop and pick out two bottles of wine — one to cook with and another to drink along with it. And make sure to use super-premium butter. Go big or go home. This is a rich, decadent splurge of a dish. Let it sing.*

INGREDIENTS

4	rib-eye steaks, about 8 ounces each
	Salt and freshly ground black pepper
3	tablespoons olive oil
1	red onion, halved and sliced
2	teaspoons red wine vinegar
1	cup dry red wine
½	cup (1 stick) unsalted butter, cut into pieces

1   Pat the steaks dry and liberally season with salt and pepper. Set aside to come to room temperature.

2   Meanwhile, heat a 12-inch cast-iron skillet (or two if you don't want to do this in batches) over high heat, until very hot.

3   Add 1 tablespoon of the oil to the pan, sprinkle on some salt, then add two of the steaks. Sear on one side for 4 minutes, turn, and cook 5 minutes longer for medium-rare, or 8 minutes for medium.

4   Remove the steaks to a plate and allow to rest, covered with a piece of foil. Cook the remaining two steaks, adding another 1 tablespoon of oil and some salt to the pan before cooking.

5   To make the sauce, lower the heat to medium and add the remaining 1 tablespoon oil, red onion, and vinegar to the skillet. Let simmer for 1 minute, then add the wine. Let simmer for 2 minutes and then reduce the heat to low. Whisking constantly, add the butter a few pieces at a time, until the sauce is thickened (you may not use all of the butter). Season to taste with salt and pepper.

6   Serve the steaks whole, or sliced into ½-inch slices, and topped with sauce.

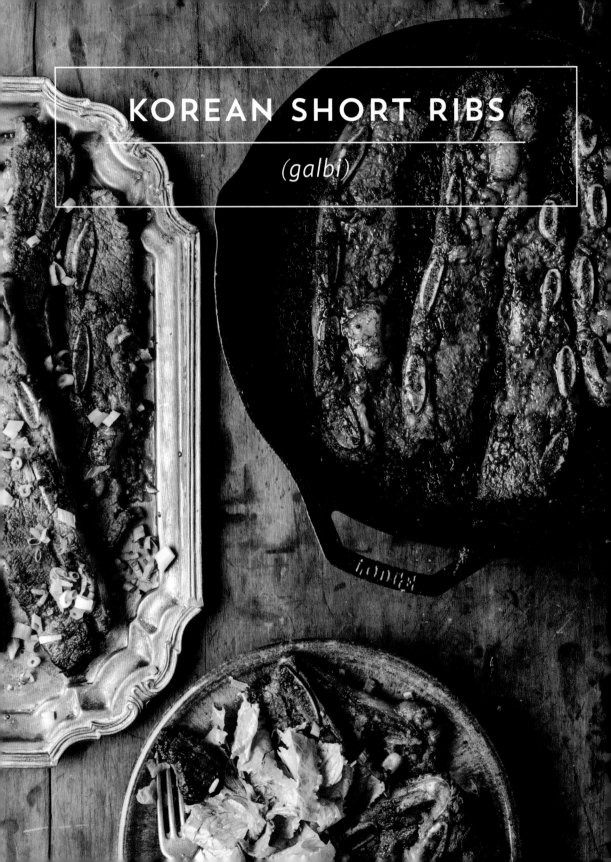

KOREAN SHORT RIBS

(galbi)

KOREAN SHORT RIBS, *or* galbi, *appeal to everyone. To serve, place a bit of the meat in a lettuce leaf, top it with extra sauce and scallions, then pop it in your mouth and repeat. After a few tries, you, too, will be crushing it, galbi-style. This recipe translates perfectly to outdoor cooking.*

INGREDIENTS

6   pounds flanken-cut beef short ribs
    Salt and freshly ground black pepper

1   cup soy sauce

¼   cup vegetable oil

⅓   cup rice wine

2   tablespoons sesame oil

¼   cup brown sugar

1   tablespoon sesame seeds

1   teaspoon red pepper flakes

1   bunch scallions, sliced, plus more
        for garnish

2   Asian pears, peeled and cored

1   onion, finely chopped

1   cup garlic cloves, peeled and trimmed

2   tablespoons chopped fresh ginger
    Cooked rice and lettuce, for serving

 Serves 4–6

1   Pat the meat dry and season with salt and pepper. Place in a shallow dish or large ziplock bag. Add the soy sauce, vegetable oil, rice wine, sesame oil, sugar, sesame seeds, red pepper flakes, and scallions to the dish (or bag).

2   Combine the pears, onion, garlic, and ginger in a food processor and process until smooth. Add the garlic mixture to the meat and stir to coat. Marinate, covered and refrigerated, for 12 to 24 hours.

3   Remove the meat from the marinade. Pour the remaining marinade into a small saucepan and bring to a simmer over very low heat.

4   Heat one or two 12-inch cast-iron skillets over medium-high heat. Once you start cooking the meat, it will smoke, so turn on your overhead fan if you have one.

5   Cook the meat in batches, turning often. When the meat is slightly charred, add a tablespoon of marinade to the pan and cook for another few minutes while it thickens into a glaze.

6   Garnish the meat with scallions. Serve with rice, torn lettuce, and additional marinade.

LUNCH & DINNER

67

FAJITAS

with steak

THESE FAJITAS *are as beautiful to look at as they are delicious to eat. What's more festive and fun than a sizzling pan full of food, ready to be devoured? If you have a cast-iron fajita pan, go ahead and use that, but it works just as well in a standard pan.*

INGREDIENTS

2-3	pounds skirt steak
	Salt
4	tablespoons black peppercorns
3	tablespoons dried oregano
2	tablespoons ground sweet paprika
1	tablespoon achiote seeds (optional)
1	tablespoon ground cumin
1	teaspoon ground allspice
½	teaspoon ground cloves
6	dried cascabel chiles (or dried chiles of your choice), stemmed and seeded
1	dried bay leaf, crushed
2	green bell peppers, cut into strips
1	large onion, sliced into thin wedges
	Flour tortillas, salsa, sour cream, and guacamole, for serving

1   Pat the meat dry and season liberally with salt.

2   In a spice mill, grind the black pepper, oregano, paprika, achiote (if using), cumin, allspice, cloves, chiles, and bay leaf. Sift into a medium bowl to remove any large pieces that didn't grind. Add enough water to create a thick paste.

3   Place the steak in a large ziplock bag, add the paste, and seal, pushing out as much air as possible. Massage the paste into the steak. Refrigerate for at least 2 hours and up to 24 hours. Turn the bag over once or twice while it's marinating.

4   Remove the steak from the refrigerator and let it come to room temperature.

5   Heat a large cast-iron grill pan or skillet. Cook the meat over high heat, turning once or twice, until desired doneness (120°F/50°C for medium-rare or 125–130°F/52–54°C for medium). Let the meat rest on a platter, tented with foil, while you cook the vegetables.

6   Add the bell peppers and onion to the pan and cook until slightly charred, about 10 minutes.

7   Slice the meat very thinly, against the grain. Toss with the vegetables and serve on flour tortillas with salsa, sour cream, and guacamole.

PARTY NUTS

---

with spices

PARTY NUTS *are a crowd-pleaser. I started entertaining at a really early age, if for no other reason than I was always bent on trying a new recipe that had caught my eye. By the time I got my first apartment, I was an expert at putting out a cocktail-hour spread that almost always included these party nuts. Use kosher salt for added texture.*

INGREDIENTS

2   cups sugar

3   cups assorted unsalted nuts (pecans, walnuts, and/or almonds)

    Pinch of ground cayenne

1   teaspoon minced fresh rosemary

1   teaspoon kosher salt

1   teaspoon freshly ground black pepper

Makes 3 cups

---

1   Line a baking sheet with parchment paper. Lightly coat the parchment with cooking spray or a thin film of vegetable oil.

2   Spread the sugar evenly in a 12-inch cast-iron pan. Cook over medium heat. As the sugar melts, use a rubber spatula to carefully begin stirring. When the sugar is melted, add the nuts, cayenne, rosemary, salt, and pepper. Stir to coat, then immediately transfer to the baking sheet and spread out as thinly as possible. Let cool completely.

FLATBREADS

perfect for dips

FLATBREADS *are so simple that once you've mastered them, they are a delightful way to play with heirloom flours. They are also super-fun to make over a campfire. Have the dough ready and place a pan on a rack over a low fire or on a cooler spot on your grill. The cooking time remains the same. Serve with eggplant dip (page 74).*

INGREDIENTS

½	cup warm water
1	packet (2¼ teaspoons) active dry yeast
2½	cups all-purpose flour
½	cup whole-wheat flour
1	teaspoon salt

1   Pour the warm water into a small bowl. Sprinkle the yeast on top and let rest for 2 minutes, until the yeast foams.

2   Add the all-purpose flour, whole-wheat flour, and salt to the bowl of a stand mixer. With the mixer on low, add the water slowly, until a smooth ball of dough forms. It should not be sticky. This can take up to 8 minutes. You may not need all the water, or you may require a bit more.

3   Place the ball of dough in a lightly oiled bowl, cover with a clean cloth, and let rise for 1 hour.

4   Remove the dough from the oiled bowl and knead briefly by hand, then divide into 12 equal-size balls. Roll out each ball of dough to a diameter of 6 inches and 1/16 inch thick.

5   Heat a dry 12-inch cast-iron skillet over high heat. Add one disk of dough and cook until lightly browned on the bottom, about 2 minutes, depending on thickness. Use tongs to turn the dough and cook for 1 minute longer. Repeat with all the dough.

6   Serve warm or store in an airtight container for up to 2 days.

SIDES & SNACKS

CHARRED EGGPLANT DIP

with tomatoes and garlic

CHARRED EGGPLANT DIP, *or* salata de vinete *(which you have to say quickly and as all one word to fit in at my house), has been made by my family for almost every occasion for as long as anyone can remember. It goes great with everything from crackers to cold pasta.*

INGREDIENTS

2   large eggplants

¼   cup olive oil

1   tablespoon red wine vinegar

3   garlic cloves, minced

¼   cup minced red onion

2   tomatoes, diced

1   cup finely chopped fresh basil

1   cup finely chopped fresh mint

1   scallion, thinly sliced

   Salt and freshly ground black pepper

Makes about 2 cups

1   Char the eggplants over an open flame or under the broiler, turning frequently, until they are blackened in spots, about 5 minutes.

2   Preheat the oven to 350°F/175°C.

3   Arrange the eggplants in a 12-inch cast-iron skillet. Place in the oven and cook for about 20 minutes, until soft. Allow to cool.

4   Scrape out the eggplant flesh and add to a food processor. Pulse until smooth. Transfer to a bowl and fold in the oil, vinegar, garlic, red onion, tomatoes, basil, mint, and scallion. Season to taste with salt and pepper. Let rest, refrigerated, for 1 hour before serving.

BRUSSELS SPROUTS

with bacon

BRUSSELS SPROUTS *have become less bitter and in turn more popular in the past few decades. Adding bacon to them certainly didn't hurt, either.*

INGREDIENTS

2   slices bacon, cut into 1-inch pieces

2   pounds Brussels sprouts, trimmed and halved lengthwise

1   red onion, sliced into thick half-moons

½   teaspoon salt

     Balsamic vinegar, for serving

Serves 4–6

1 In a 10- or 12-inch cast-iron skillet, cook the bacon over medium heat until crisp. Remove the bacon to a paper towel–lined plate to drain.

2 Stir the Brussels sprouts and onion in the remaining fat and add the salt. Cook over medium-low heat, turning once or twice, until just tender and browned, 20 to 25 minutes.

3 Meanwhile, chop the bacon.

4 Sprinkle the sprouts with the bacon and a dash of vinegar to serve.

CARROTS & PARSNIPS

with chimichurri

CARROTS & PARSNIPS WITH CHIMICHURRI *may steal your heart. Eating in Argentina means falling in love with chimichurri, a wonderfully ubiquitous condiment found on every table. Smaller, whole carrots — such as the Icicle variety — in a variety of colors are beautiful in this dish, but if you can't find whole carrots that will fit in your pan, trim larger carrots.*

CHIMICHURRI

1	cup minced fresh parsley
2	tablespoons minced fresh oregano
2	garlic cloves, minced
¾	cup olive oil
¼	cup red wine vinegar
	Large pinch of red pepper flakes
	Salt

VEGETABLES

2	tablespoons butter
1	tablespoon olive oil
1½	pounds small, whole carrots, trimmed
1½	pounds small parsnips, trimmed
1	tablespoon roughly chopped almonds
	Salt

 Serves 4–6

1   To make the chimichurri, combine the parsley, oregano, garlic, oil, vinegar, and red pepper flakes in a large bowl. Let rest for at least 30 minutes. Season with salt to taste. This recipe will make 2 cups of chimichurri; leftovers will keep in the fridge for up to 5 days.

2   In the meantime, for the vegetables, melt the butter in a 10- or 12-inch cast-iron skillet over medium heat. Add the oil and heat for 30 seconds.

3   Add the carrots and parsnips, stirring gently to coat. Cook, turning often, until the vegetables are softened and browned, about 6 minutes. Toss in the almonds and salt to taste and stir to coat.

4   Remove the vegetables from the pan and allow to cool slightly. Serve hot or at room temperature, with ½ cup of chimichurri spooned over.

PERSIAN RICE

crispy and delicious

PERSIAN RICE *is really two things: the rice itself and the* tahdig *— the intentionally crispy rice from the bottom of the pan. To get the right results for this rice, make sure to follow the directions exactly and use a seasoned cast-iron (not enameled) pan. You'll need cheesecloth to make this dish. Serve with kebabs, lamb stew, or a salad of salted tomatoes and raw onion.*

INGREDIENTS

8	cups water
2	cups white basmati rice
1	tablespoon salt
3	tablespoons coconut oil
3	strands saffron, ground, or 1 teaspoon ground turmeric

Makes 5½ cups rice

1   Pour the rice into a large bowl and add enough water to cover. Let soak for 1 hour, then drain and rinse several times to remove any additional starch.

2   Boil the 8 cups water in a large cast-iron Dutch oven. Add the rice and salt and boil, cooking until the rice is slightly undercooked (6 to 8 minutes), stirring occasionally. Drain, then rinse with cold water to remove excess starch.

3   Heat the oil in the Dutch oven over low heat. Add the saffron and stir.

4   Immediately add about 2 cups of the cooked rice in an even layer, pressing down with a spoon to compact it.

5   Pile the remaining rice on top in a mound. Using a chopstick or spoon handle, make a hole in the center of the mound to allow the steam to escape. Top with cheesecloth, making sure the cheesecloth touches the rice.

6   Cover the pan with foil, then a lid, and cook over low heat for 50 minutes, rotating the pot a few times to ensure even cooking. To serve, invert the entire pan onto a platter, or gently scoop out the cooked rice, then loosen the sides of the tahdig with an offset spatula. Serve whole or broken in pieces.

CORN BREAD

two ways

Sweet & Light
Corn Bread

CORN BREAD *has been made in as many versions as there are stars in the sky. There's Northern, which is sweet, and Southern, which is typically made with white corn. Then there's Southwestern-style, with chiles and fresh corn kernels; and the list goes on. Here I present two variations: a "sweet and light" version that is light and cakey, and a "dense and intense" option that is perfect for drowning in buttermilk and eating with a spoon.*

SWEET & LIGHT CORN BREAD

3	cups all-purpose flour
1½	cups fine cornmeal
1½	cups sugar
2	teaspoons baking powder
1	teaspoon baking soda
1½	teaspoons salt
5	eggs
2	cups milk
½	cup vegetable oil
2	tablespoons butter

DENSE & INTENSE CORN BREAD

2½	cups medium-grind cornmeal
1	cup all-purpose flour
2	tablespoons sugar (optional)
1	tablespoon kosher salt
2½	teaspoons baking powder
2	tablespoons vegetable oil

Serves 4–6

Sweet & Light Corn Bread

1   Place a 12-inch cast-iron skillet in the oven on the middle rack and preheat to 350°F/175°C.

2   In a large bowl, stir together the flour, cornmeal, sugar, baking powder, baking soda, and salt. Set aside.

3   Separate the eggs, putting the yolks in a large bowl and the whites in a medium bowl. Add the milk and oil to the yolks and stir to combine. Using a hand mixer or a whisk, whip the whites until they hold a medium peak.

4   Meanwhile, remove the pan from the oven and add the butter. Return the pan to the oven to melt the butter.

5   Stir the egg yolk mixture into the dry ingredients. Gently fold the egg whites into the batter until just combined. Pour the batter into the pan and return it to the oven for 40 to 55 minutes, or until a toothpick inserted into the center comes out clean. Cool in the pan, slice, and serve.

Dense & Intense Corn Bread

1   Preheat the oven to 350°F/175°C.

2   Combine the cornmeal, flour, sugar (if using), salt, and baking powder in a large bowl. Add the oil and enough water to form a loose batter.

3   Pour into a well-oiled 10-inch cast-iron skillet. Bake for 30 to 45 minutes, or until a toothpick inserted into the center comes out clean. The bread will be dense and dark golden brown. Serve warm.

BAKED APPLES

with walnuts

BAKED APPLES *are like heaven in a bowl. My mother believed in feeding us well, and that meant few decadent desserts. When we did indulge, it was usually with these huge warm apples, bubbling with butter and melted sugar. Serve with ice cream or a glass of milk.*

INGREDIENTS

4	large baking apples (Rome or Honeycrisp works well)
½	cup (1 stick) butter, softened
1	cup brown sugar
¼	cup chopped walnuts

Makes 4 apples

1 Stem and partially core the apples, being careful not to make a hole all the way through.

2 In a large bowl, mix together half the butter and half the sugar. Stuff the apples with the butter-sugar mixture and top with walnuts.

3 Melt the rest of the butter and sugar in a cast-iron Dutch oven or skillet with a lid.

4 Nestle the apples in the pan and cover. Cook over medium-low heat for 30 to 45 minutes, or until soft.

Note: *For cooking outdoors, line the Dutch oven with two pieces of heavy-duty aluminum foil, then place the oven on a grate over a low fire.*

HOT & SPICY GINGERBREAD

with white pepper

HOT & SPICY GINGERBREAD *is a Caribbean-style bread that's rich and moist and has a lot of deep heat from the combination of ginger and white pepper. Making it in a cast-iron pan will add an extra-dark, beautifully robust exterior, which pairs flawlessly with a glass of sparkling cider, ginger beer, or chai.*

INGREDIENTS

1½ cups all-purpose flour

2 teaspoons ground ginger

1 teaspoon ground allspice

1 teaspoon ground cinnamon

1 teaspoon ground white pepper

½ teaspoon ground mace

1 teaspoon baking powder

½ teaspoon baking soda

½ teaspoon salt

½ cup (1 stick) butter, at room temperature

½ cup firmly packed dark brown sugar

¼ cup granulated sugar

1 egg

½ cup molasses

½ cup warm water

¼ cup grated fresh ginger

1 Preheat the oven to 350°F/175°C. Grease a 10-inch cast-iron skillet with butter.

2 In a large bowl, whisk together the flour, ground ginger, allspice, cinnamon, white pepper, mace, baking powder, baking soda, and salt.

3 Place the butter and sugars in a large bowl. Using a stand mixer or hand mixer, cream on high speed until fluffy, about 3 minutes. Lower the speed to medium, add the egg, and mix until incorporated. Add the molasses and mix until incorporated.

4 Reduce the mixer speed to low and add one-third of the flour mixture. Add ¼ cup of the warm water and mix. Add another third of the flour, then the remaining ¼ cup warm water. Finish with the remaining flour (it's important to end with the flour).

5 Using a spatula, fold in the grated ginger, then pour into the prepared skillet.

6 Bake for about 40 minutes, until a toothpick inserted into the center comes out clean. Remove from the oven and let cool for 20 minutes. Serve warm or at room temperature.

S'MORES

oven-style

THESE S'MORES *are perfect for when you don't have an open fire and a bunch of sticks. Make sure to keep an eye on the marshmallows when they are broiling; you don't want them to get too dark.*

INGREDIENTS

2	cups finely chopped chocolate (or use chocolate chips)
2	tablespoons butter
12	plain graham crackers, broken into pieces
14–20	large marshmallows

Serves 4–6

1   Preheat the broiler.

2   Place the chocolate and butter in a 10-inch cast-iron skillet and melt over very low heat. Using a wooden spoon, stir until smooth. Do not let the chocolate scorch. Remove from the heat and allow to cool for 4 minutes.

3   Arrange the graham crackers on top of the chocolate, then top with a single layer of marshmallows.

4   Place the skillet under the broiler and roast, keeping an eye on the pan, until the marshmallows are browned. Serve family-style or scoop out into individual bowls.

PEACH CRISP

easy and divine

PEACH CRISP, *with its crumble topping, is perfect for celebrating life's imperfect, messy moments. It's warming and kind and can be put together in minutes. When scooped, it's not going to be picture-perfect, but the taste sure is divine.*

Serves 4–6

INGREDIENTS

5   large peaches, pitted and sliced
    ¼ inch thick

1   teaspoon ground cinnamon

½   teaspoon ground nutmeg

1   cup plus 2 tablespoons all-purpose flour

¼   cup granulated sugar

1   cup rolled oats

⅓   cup firmly packed light brown sugar

5   tablespoons butter, cut into pieces and
    softened

1   Preheat the oven to 350°F/175°C.

2   In a medium bowl, gently toss the peaches with the cinnamon, nutmeg, 2 tablespoons of the flour, and granulated sugar.

3   To make the topping, combine the oats, brown sugar, butter, and the remaining 1 cup flour in a separate bowl. Mix with your hands until it just comes together.

4   Transfer the peaches to a 10-inch cast-iron skillet and scatter the topping over them. Place the skillet on a baking sheet to catch any overflow. Bake for 30 to 40 minutes, or until the topping is browned. Serve warm.

CRANBERRY UPSIDE-DOWN CAKE

with fresh or frozen berries

CRANBERRY UPSIDE-DOWN CAKE *is a visually stunning, gemlike dessert — or breakfast — that can be made any time of the year. The basic upside-down cake works just as well with fresh or frozen cranberries. If you use frozen, don't even bother defrosting; they can just be poured right into the pan.*

INGREDIENTS

1½   cups (3 sticks) butter

1   cup firmly packed brown sugar

2   cups cranberries, fresh or frozen

2½   cups all-purpose flour

1½   teaspoons baking powder

¼   teaspoon baking soda

     Pinch of salt

2   cups granulated sugar

     Zest of 1 orange

3   eggs

1   cup whole milk

Serves 6–8

1   Preheat the oven to 350°F/175°C.

2   Melt ½ cup of the butter and the brown sugar in a 10-inch cast-iron skillet over medium heat. Remove from the heat and add the cranberries. Set aside.

3   Combine the flour, baking powder, baking soda, and salt in a large bowl and whisk together. Set aside.

4   In another bowl, combine the granulated sugar, orange zest, and remaining 1 cup butter, and blend until light and fluffy, about 3 minutes. Add the eggs one at a time and mix until incorporated.

5   With an electric mixer on low speed, add one-third the flour mixture to the batter, then add one-third of the milk. Alternate adding the flour and milk, and mix until the batter is smooth.

6   Pour the batter over the cranberries. Place the skillet on a baking sheet to catch any spillover and set in the oven. Bake for about 30 minutes, or until the top is golden and a toothpick inserted into the center comes out clean.

7   Let the cake cool for 10 minutes before slicing into wedges to serve.

INDEX

Page numbers in *italic* indicate photos.

KEEP YOUR

Creativity Cooking

WITH MORE BOOKS
from Storey

These and other books from Storey Publishing are available wherever quality books are sold or by calling 1-800-441-5700. Visit us at *www.storey.com* or sign up for our newsletter at *www.storey.com/signup*.

OLWEN WOODIER

Apple pie is just the beginning! Discover the versatility of this iconic fruit with 125 delicious recipes for any meal, including apple frittata, pork chops with apple cream sauce, apple pizza, apple butter, and much more.

- - - - - - - - - - - - - - - -

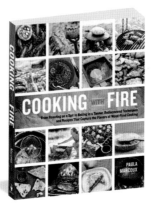

PAULA MARCOUX

Rediscover timeless techniques and exciting new ones — from roasting on a spit to baking in a masonry oven — with this comprehensive guide to all the tools, instructions, and recipes you'll need to master wood-fired cooking.

- - - - - - - - - - - - - - - -

JENNIFER TRAINER THOMPSON

Crack open this wealth of ideas for using eggs from local farms and your own backyard. Make the most of your eggs with delicious menu-spanning recipes, including eggnog, huevos rancheros, zucchini fritters, lemon mousse, and more.

- - - - - - - - - - - - - - - -

MAGGIE STUCKEY

Bring the neighborhood together with your own soup night, choosing from 90 crowd-pleasing recipes for hearty chowders, chilis, and vegetable soups for any time of year. Additional recipes for salads, breads, and dessert round out the soup night experience.